iced tea

iced tea

50 RECIPES FOR
REFRESHING
TISANES,
INFUSIONS,
COOLERS, AND
SPIKED TEAS

FRED THOMPSON

THE HARVARD COMMON PRESS
BOSTON, MASSACHUSETTS

For Laura, live your life well

THE HARVARD COMMON PRESS
535 Albany Street
Boston, Massachusetts 02118
www.harvardcommonpress.com

Printed in China
Printed on acid-free paper

Library of Congress Cataloging-in-Publication Data

Thompson, Fred
  Iced Tea : 50 cool recipes for refreshing tisanes, infusions, coolers, and spiked teas /
  by Fred Thompson
    p. cm.
  ISBN 1-55832-228-0 (cl : alk. paper)
    1. Iced tea. 2. Herbal teas. I. Title.
TX817.T3 T48 2002
641.6'372–dc21

                                                    2001051539

10 9 8 7 6 5 4 3 2

Jacket and interior design by Elizabeth Van Itallie
Photographs on pages 15, 50, 58, 70, and 80 by Elizabeth Van Itallie

Jacket recipe: Twisted *Joy of Cooking* Iced Tea, page 22

contents

Iced tea.

Iced tea. Who could have imagined the explosion that has changed "the house wine of the South" into a national phenomenon? Once a summer-only beverage in much of the country, iced tea has elevated itself to a year-round refresher. Even in New York City, where iced tea was once frowned upon, restaurants are learning how to make and serve it.

Tea has been around for almost five thousand years and is the second most popular beverage, after water, in the world. Dutchman Peter Stuyvesant generally gets the credit for introducing tea to North America around 1650. Tea took off in the Dutch colony of New Amsterdam (now that little place called New York City), and drinking tea was widespread in the 1700s.

Like so many things in the food world, iced tea was the product of necessity and desperation. The 1904 World's Fair in St. Louis was America's coming-out party. One of the exhibitors was a gentleman tea plantation owner named Richard Blechynden, who arrived at the fair set on giving away free samples of tea. Hot tea. During the fair's run, St. Louis had a miserable heat wave. Concerned that his efforts and monetary investment at the fair were doomed, he did what any Southerner takes for granted today: he added bags of ice to his hot tea. The story, which seems to show up in all the histories of tea, claims that his iced tea was one of the great masterstrokes of the fair. But, then, Jack Daniel's Old No. 7 took home a gold medal, too. Southerners, it seems, had a good run in St. Louis.

Growing up in the South, I watched grandmothers, aunts, and my mother "make tea," which, in the South, means iced tea. The different versions of iced tea I consumed at home, family reunions, church suppers, and restaurants all had subtle variations in taste. My mother's, of course, was always the best, but all had three things in common: a dark amber hue, copious amounts of sugar, and being made with care. Though not sacred, good iced tea is con-

6

sidered essential to a Southerner's happiness and well-being. The importance of iced tea can best be illustrated by this old Southern saying: "In the South, never marry a man until you know how to make his mama's tea." And I, having been transplanted part of each year to Manhattan, make a ritual of bringing Luzianne family-size tea bags with me from North Carolina to ensure that I have quality tea.

Iced tea has always been a part of my life. Never would you find Mom's refrigerator lacking iced tea. A major passage to adulthood came on the day I was allowed to trade milk for iced tea with a meal. The hardest part about writing this book has been typing "iced tea." In the South it is "ice tea." Like barbecue, Southerners have taken the action out of the process. You will find many restaurant menus still listing "ice tea."

As iced tea has swept across America, I fear that we are developing the taste for artificial ingredients, additives, and unnatural color. Although some of the convenience tea products are pretty good (especially those in the milk case), none can live up to a homebrewed glass of iced tea. It takes only 15 to 20 minutes to make—how convenient is that?

the
basics

To make good iced tea, you should follow a few simple principles, techniques, and rules. None of this is rocket science, and even with a mistake here and there, you'll still have a better glass of iced tea than those that come from cans and powders. I've also thrown in some history, which once again shows that desperation can be the mother of invention. Two components always have to come together for there to be tea: tea leaves, obviously, and water.

tea

There are three types of tea from which to choose: black, green, and oolong.

BLACK TEA

Ninety percent of the tea consumed in the world is black tea. Orange pekoe? Black tea. Those tiny little tea leaves? Black tea. Black tea goes through a total oxidation (fermentation) process before being heated and dried. Black tea has an almost mahogany color and a bright taste. To most of us, this is tea.

GREEN TEA

Green tea goes through no fermentation process, making for a lightly colored tea with a delicate flavor.

OOLONG TEA

The preferred tea in Asia, oolong is fermented somewhere between black and green tea. Still brown in color, oolong has a luxurious, smoky, almost peachy flavor. Some of the most famous and sought-after teas are oolong.

There is another category of "tea"—tisanes. These are teas made not from tea leaves, but from flowers, herbs, and spices, such as chamomile or rose hips. Many claim certain curative properties. Once confined to health food stores, tisanes are now more widely available.

Growing tea is much like producing wine. The same type of tea shrub grown in different climates and soils will have different flavor characteristics in the final dried leaves. What we see on grocery store shelves are teas blended from various regions.

There's another similarity between wine and tea: both have noted health benefits. Tea's health benefits seem to get rediscovered every half century. Black, oolong, and green tea go after those pesky free radicals with flavonoid antioxidants. The consumption of tea has also been linked to lower instances of cancer and stroke. Sounds like a great deal: healing refreshment.

So which tea gets the nod for iced tea? There are many tea brands in your local supermarket. Luzianne has long been considered the iced tea champion, because it is blended especially for iced tea. If you have access to Luzianne, by all means use it. Lipton was my mother's tea of choice, and I've found Tetley to have a wonderful flavor. American Classic Tea, which is produced in the United States, makes a full-bodied iced tea. Look for it in gourmet stores. Call me old-fashioned, but I haven't taken to the cold-brew teas on the market. Twinings, Bigelow, and even Lipton produce good flavored teas. Tazo and Celestial Seasonings have interesting teas. Let your taste guide you.

Most of the recipes in this book call for regular-size tea bags. Regular-size bags give you much more versatility, are available everywhere, and come in more options and flavors (there may be an Earl Grey family-size bag in England, but I've never seen one in a retail store). When making two quarts of iced tea with family-size tea bags, a ratio of one family-size to every three regular-size bags generally will work.

If you keep tea in the pantry, you'll be ready for that first heat wave. You should always have black tea, especially an orange pekoe blend, on hand. Green tea is a nice diversion. I try to keep a few flavored teas around. They can make unexpected company feel special. Peach-, raspberry-, and mint-flavored teas are good choices. I also keep black currant tea in my pantry just because I like it.

water

Water has a major impact on tea. If you live in an area where water is chemically treated and you can smell or taste the chemicals, use bottled or filtered water. Good water brews good tea.

In my recipes, I bring water to a gentle boil and add the tea bags to the water. Most other recipes suggest pouring the boiling water over the tea. Suit yourself; I like having as few things to wash as possible. With my method, you might have to add a few ounces of cold water at the end to make up for evaporation.

six rules for making good iced tea

The single most tragic mistake in preparing iced tea is not making it strong enough. What tastes right when warm will taste different cold. Which leads me to my first rule.

RULE 1

Start with enough tea bags. Following most producers' instructions will lead to wimpy iced tea. Try my methods for brewing the various teas at least once, then you decide.

RULE 2

To strengthen your tea, add more tea bags (or loose tea); don't lengthen the steeping time. Allowing tea to oversteep brings out its bitterness, making the tannins more pronounced. For weaker tea, reduce the steeping time rather than removing any tea bags. Start with about a two-minute reduction.

RULE 3

I am a Southerner, and even though I live part-time in Manhattan, I have held to certain Southern truths. New Yorkers may have taught me to walk fast, but they have not altered my taste for sweets. You may need to adjust the sweetness levels in some of the recipes. On the topic of sweets, most of my recipes call for granulated sugar or other types of sugar. Honey, stevia, or artificial sweeteners can be substituted. Splenda, a new sugar substitute, is excellent in iced tea; even Consumers Union likes this product.

Some folks use sugar syrup when making a pitcher of iced tea. Feel free to try it with any of my tea recipes, adding it to taste.

RULE 4

Putting hot tea in a cold refrigerator will guarantee cloudy tea. Let your tea cool before refrigerating it. Adding some boiling water to cloudy tea will save the day—sometimes.

RULE 5

Keep your iced tea fresh. Make only what you can drink in two to three days.

RULE 6

Never, ever use anything but freshly squeezed lemon juice. Frozen lemon juice is passable in an emergency. Why ruin your fresh-tasting tea with an artificial flavor?

sugar syrup

In upscale restaurants in metropolitan areas across the country, sugar syrup is routinely delivered along with your unsweetened iced tea. This beats the heck out of battling with sugar to sweeten your tea. No matter how long you stir (not to mention the noise of that teaspoon banging against the glass and the ice), you can never get it to dissolve. This syrup also offers a solution when multiple opinions on sweetness are about.

1 1/2 cups cold water
1 cup granulated sugar

1. In a small saucepan, combine the water and sugar. Stir over low heat until the sugar is dissolved. You can tell: the gritty sound stops.

2. Bring to a boil, reduce the heat to a simmer, and cook for about 10 minutes. The mixture should be syrupy. It also will be very hot, so be careful. Let cool. Pour into steeped tea or other libations. Refrigerated sugar syrup will keep for about a month, tightly covered.

➤ MAKES ABOUT 1 CUP

serving iced tea

Serving iced tea in the South can be an elegant affair: crystal pitchers glistening with condensation, tall glasses filled with ice cubes at the ready, and a side dish with lemon wedges. What a moment. Do you need all this for great iced tea? Not really. Tea seems to taste better when stored in a glass container, but that is really splitting hairs. Plastic works fine. Transferring tea into a nice glass pitcher to serve is a nice touch. I do like tall glasses as opposed to old-fashioned glasses. They are easier to sip from without having to fight the ice. Mason jars work fine, too. This is one of the reasons I give many of the yields in total amounts rather than servings. The size of the glass, the amount of ice, and what the tea is being used for all factor into the number of servings. Six to eight ounces is about average per serving, with punch cups being three to five ounces.

Lemon wedges don't need to be huge. If you're using a medium-size lemon, cut it into eight wedges. This will supply a nice burst of lemon flavor without overpowering the tea. Don't serve lemon when you are serving a flavored tea or punch.

Those long iced-tea spoons are great for stirring in sweetener or distributing lemon juice. Don't leave a person without some sort of spoon that can be dedicated to the tea. (Iced-tea spoons are also great for getting the last of the mayonnaise out of the jar.)

Tea is a beverage few people dislike, which makes it perfect for all types of occasions. Maybe because iced tea's been so long associated with the South, it seems to slow us down and gives us a chance to catch our breath, if only for a moment. A glass of iced tea is always welcome.

This book is full of elegant, fun, and basic recipes designed to stimulate your palate. I encourage you to try several, then use them as a springboard for your own concoctions. Let me know what you discover. And enjoy the sociability of iced tea.

the
classics

There is definitely more than one way to make iced tea, and this chapter will give you a couple. The main point in making the classics is making the tea strong enough to hold its flavor once chilled and iced. Besides the every-day Southern-style tea, I have also included some not-so-everyday teas such as green and oolong. "High tea" is not the sole domain for loose tea leaves. Loose tea also can be used to add many subtle nuances of flavor.

southern-style iced tea

There are as many ways to brew iced tea as there are Southern grandmothers. I grew up on iced tea made by bringing a small amount of water to a slow boil and then pouring it over the tea bags to form a concentrate. More water is added to finish the process. I guess I'm biased toward this method, but it definitely makes good tea. The baking soda might seem strange, but it softens the natural tannins that cause an acid or bitter taste.

6 regular-size tea bags

$1/8$ teaspoon baking soda (a good pinch)

2 cups boiling water

6 cups cold water

Granulated sugar or other sweetener to taste (optional)

1. In a glass measuring cup or ceramic teapot large enough to accommodate the boiling water, place the tea bags and baking soda. Pour the boiling water over the tea bags. Cover and let steep for 15 minutes.

2. Remove the tea bags, being careful not to squeeze them (squeezing the bags will add bitterness).

3. Pour the concentrate into a 2-quart pitcher and add the cold water. Sweeten, if desired.

4. Let cool, then chill and serve over ice.

➤ MAKES 2 QUARTS

Tea will become cloudy if refrigerated while still warm. Add a little boiling water to clear up the cloudiness.

The tannins in tea also cause cloudiness when the tea is brewed in hard water. If you know you have minerals in your water, use bottled or filtered water.

loose-leaf
cold brew

For variety, try this method. With the multitude of loose tea leaves available, you might just discover iced tea utopia.

1 gallon cold water

3 tablespoons tea leaves (any type: black currant is a good start)

1 cup superfine sugar (optional), or to taste

1. Fill a 1-gallon container with the cold water. Add the tea leaves, cover tightly, and shake to combine. Let sit overnight in the refrigerator or place in full sunlight for 3 to 4 hours.

2. Strain through a fine-mesh strainer into a clean container and stir in the sugar (if using) until it dissolves.

3. Chill and serve over ice.

➤ MAKES 1 GALLON

With a cold-brew method, superfine sugar, sometimes called bartenders' sugar, dissolves more quickly and thoroughly than regular granulated sugar. Sugar Syrup (page 13) also can be used.

Cold-brew methods decrease the amount of caffeine pulled out of the tea leaves.

low-country iced tea

The Low Country is officially the area between Charleston, South Carolina, and Savannah, Georgia. But several other coastal areas, even parts of the Grand Strand of Myrtle Beach, now consider themselves part of the Low Country. This style of making iced tea is similar to making a big teapot of hot tea, so you will need a large heatproof pitcher.

6 regular-size tea bags

6 cups boiling water

$1/4$ cup freshly squeezed lemon juice (about 1 $1/2$ lemons; don't even think of using bottled)

$1/4$ cup granulated sugar

1. Place the tea bags in a large heatproof pitcher. Pour the boiling water over the tea bags. Let steep for 3 to 5 minutes, longer for stronger tea.

2. Remove the tea bags without squeezing them. Add the lemon juice and sugar and stir to combine.

3. Let cool, then chill and serve over ice.

➤ MAKES ABOUT 1½ QUARTS

sweet tea, aka "the house wine of the south"

The South would secede from the Union again if sweet tea were banned from our borders. No self-respecting barbecue house or fish camp would ever stop serving sweet tea. Most, for many years, gave no option but sweet tea, and the righteously committed still serve only the sugary brew. And sweet it is. A visitor to the South once said that it made his teeth hurt. Why so sweet? In general, Southerners just have a big sweet tooth, but an "unidentified source" who owns a famous North Carolina barbecue house once confided, "The sugar makes the tea go farther, and it used to be that the sugar was cheaper than the tea." In truth, I always thought it was to cut the vinegar-based barbecue sauce or round out the fried flavor of our favorite foods. Whatever the reason, once adopted, Southern sweet tea is hard to give up.

6 regular-size tea bags
$^1/_8$ teaspoon baking soda (a good pinch)
2 cups boiling water
$1^1/_2$ to 2 cups granulated sugar (if you are new to sweet tea, start with $1^1/_4$ cups)
6 cups cold water

1. In a glass measuring cup or ceramic teapot large enough to accommodate the boiling water, place the tea bags and baking soda. Pour the boiling water over the tea bags. Cover and let steep for 15 minutes.

2. Remove the tea bags, being careful not to squeeze them (squeezing the bags will add bitterness).

3. Pour the concentrate into a 2-quart pitcher and add the sugar. Stir until almost dissolved. Stir in the cold water.

4. Let cool, then chill and serve over ice.

➤ MAKES 2 QUARTS

twisted *joy of cooking* iced tea

The *Joy of Cooking* cookbook has inspired many a cook, but the author's method for iced tea needed some tweaking.

> $^{1}/_{4}$ cup tea leaves (any type)
>
> 4 cups boiling water
>
> Granulated sugar to taste (optional)
>
> Fresh mint sprigs for garnish
>
> Lemon wedges for garnish

1. Place the tea leaves in a heatproof container. Pour the boiling water over the tea, cover, and let steep for 3 to 5 minutes. With this method, 5 minutes really is the max, and most teas seem to have a better flavor after about 4 minutes.

2. Strain through a fine-mesh strainer into a pitcher. Add sugar, if desired, stirring well to dissolve.

3. Let cool, then chill. Serve over ice, garnished with a mint sprig and lemon wedge.

➤ MAKES 1 QUART

solar tea

Let the sun shine in. To me, this is a throwback to the seventies and the days of tie-dye. But tie-dye is back, and considering the pace our world moves at today, saving even a little time can be a godsend. By the way, this also can be done by the light of the moon, and there are claims that "moon" tea has less caffeine.

3 family-size tea bags
1 gallon cold water

1. Place the tea bags in a 1-gallon container. Add the water. Put the container out in the sun for 3 to 4 hours.

2. Chill and serve over ice.

➤ MAKES 1 GALLON

For a half gallon, use 2 family-size tea bags and a half gallon of water. Steep in the sun for 2 to 3 hours.

iced green tea

Green tea has been getting a lot of positive press lately. It seems that it may be really good for us, fighting all those free radicals. Iced green tea is delicious and marries well with food. This is not as sweet as most grocery store refrigerated green teas, so you might want to adjust the honey or add some sugar. Also try a mix of green tea and wild sweet orange tea.

8 cups cold water

8 regular-size green tea bags

$^3/_4$ cup honey

$^1/_2$ cup turbinado or granulated sugar (optional)

1 teaspoon freshly squeezed lemon juice (don't use bottled)

1. Bring 2 cups of the water to a slow boil in a small saucepan. Add the tea bags, cover, and remove from the heat. Let steep for 12 to 15 minutes, depending on the desired strength.

2. Remove the tea bags without squeezing them. Add the honey, sugar (if using), and lemon juice, stirring to combine.

3. Pour into a 2-quart container and add the remaining 6 cups cold water.

4. Chill and serve over ice.

➤ MAKES ABOUT 2 QUARTS

oolong iced tea

Oolong tea is considered by some to be the Lafite Rothschild of teas. The very best comes from Taiwan. You might think that this tea is unsuitable or too cultured for iced tea, but for a special occasion, the smoky flavor notes are an interesting change. As a variation, substitute two or three peach-flavored black tea bags for an equal amount of the oolong. Oolong has a faint peach tone that can be enhanced by combining the two teas.

8 cups cold water
8 regular-size oolong tea bags
$1/4$ to $1/2$ cup granulated sugar, to your taste
Milk or lemon wedges (optional)

1. In a small saucepan, bring 2 cups of the water to a boil. Add the tea bags, cover, and remove from the heat. Let steep for 8 to 10 minutes.

2. In a 2-quart heatproof container, combine the sugar and the remaining 6 cups cold water. Pour in the tea concentrate, stirring or shaking until the sugar is dissolved.

3. Let cool, then chill until very cold. Serve over ice with milk or lemon wedges if desired.

➤ MAKES 2 QUARTS

verla's tea

Who says the North and South can't come to an agreement on iced tea? My foodie friend down the hall in Manhattan, Verla Gabriel, suggested a tea combination that I thought was interesting. "Three parts Earl Grey and one part Irish breakfast is my favorite," she said. With that as a starting point, I did a little playing around. I remembered an iced tea served in a Raleigh, North Carolina, café called the Upper Crust. A blissful place for lunch, the café served a raspberry-flavored tea. So, with a thought from Verla and a memory from Raleigh, an iced tea emerged that is second to none.

8 cups cold water, or more if needed

2 regular-size Earl Grey tea bags

2 regular-size Irish breakfast tea bags

2 regular-size raspberry-flavored tea bags

1/2 cup granulated sugar

1. In a small saucepan, bring 2 cups of the water to a gentle boil. Add all the tea bags, cover, and remove from the heat. Let steep for 10 minutes.

2. Remove the tea bags without squeezing them.

3. Pour the hot tea concentrate into a 2-quart heatproof container. Add the sugar and the remaining 6 cups cold water. Add more water, if needed, to make 2 quarts. Stir or shake until the sugar is dissolved.

4. Let cool, then chill and serve very cold over ice.

➤ MAKES 2 QUARTS

This ratio of one part Earl Grey, one part Irish breakfast, and one part raspberry-flavored tea gives the exquisite hint of raspberry without being overpowering or clashing with any food it might be served with. Peach, mint, or even a mixed-berry green tea works famously instead of the raspberry. If you want more of the flavor to be apparent, add an additional flavored tea bag and leave out one Irish breakfast bag.

fruit jug sweet tea

Sometimes you just have to make a recipe fit the right size jug. Apple juice and other fruit juice containers are perfect when recycled into tea jugs. These containers are always a funny size, such as 48 ounces. Here's a recipe that fits that size and is another variation on the sweet tea that is found in central South Carolina and Georgia. In those regions, lemon juice is added while the tea is still hot or, in some cases, even steeped with the tea bags. The recipe is an adaptation of two recipes, one from Dori Sanders, the wonderful South Carolinian cook, and one from Atlanta's great Junior League cookbook, *True Grits*. By the way, I love this recipe.

> 5 cups cold water
>
> 3 regular-size tea bags or 1 family-size tea bag
>
> 1 1/2 cups granulated sugar
>
> 1/3 cup freshly squeezed lemon juice (about 2 lemons; no bottled stuff, please)

1. Bring 2 cups of the water to just the beginning of a boil in a small saucepan. Add the tea bags, cover, and remove from the heat. Let steep for 5 minutes.

2. Remove the tea bags without squeezing them.

3. Put the sugar in a jug or pitcher. Cool the steeped tea slightly, then add it to the sugar. Stir or shake until the sugar is dissolved. Add the remaining 3 cups cold water and stir or shake to blend.

4. Let cool, then chill and serve over ice.

➤ MAKES 1 1/2 QUARTS

bahamian iced tea

In an effort to keep my sixteen-year-old daughter from going off with a bunch of high schoolers over spring break, I bribed her with a trip to the Bahamas. I also learned something new about tea.

The Bahamians like their tea both hot and cold, having been influenced by the British. Their brew method is unusual. But when the natives really want a kicking iced tea, they choose Goombay Iced Tea (page 90). This recipe can be easily multiplied.

³/₄ to 1 cup cold water

1 regular-size tea bag

4 or 5 fresh mint leaves (black spearmint is nice)

Crushed or cracked ice

Lemon wedge for garnish

1. Bring the water to a gentle boil. Pour it over the tea bag in a teacup and let steep for 5 minutes.

2. Bruise the mint leaves in the bottom of a tall glass with a long spoon. Fill the glass with crushed or cracked ice; don't use whole cubes. Pour the steeped tea over the ice. Let the ingredients meld for a minute, then top with a lemon wedge.

➤ MAKES 1 SERVING

iced
tisanes
and
infusions

Now that we have the classics, it's time to have some fun. Iced tea blends well with other good things. Just as lemon gives iced tea a lift, so do many other citrus juices, as do herbs and spices such as mint, cloves, and cinnamon. Some of these upscale iced teas take a few more minutes to make, and some are just dead simple. You'll probably find a twist on tea that will become your home's classic iced tea.

almond tea

Almonds and almond extract are mainstay seasonings in the South, so it seemed natural to test this flavor with tea. The result is a tea that enhances a meal of grilled foods or that can be served as an engaging nonalcoholic apéritif.

8 cups cold water
9 regular-size tea bags or 3 family-size tea bags
1 cup granulated sugar
1 teaspoon pure vanilla extract
1 1/2 teaspoons pure almond extract
Juice of 3 lemons

1. Bring 2 cups of the water to a slow boil in a small saucepan. Add the tea bags, cover, and remove from the heat. Let steep for 10 minutes.

2. Remove the tea bags without squeezing them.

3. Pour the steeped tea into a 2-quart heatproof container. Add the sugar and stir or shake until dissolved. Add the vanilla, almond extract, and lemon juice and stir or shake to combine. Add the remaining 6 cups cold water and stir.

4. Let cool, then chill and serve over ice.

➤ MAKES ABOUT 2 QUARTS

cinnamon iced tea

There are myriad flavored teas on the market. In one New York City gourmet shop, I counted more than 200 flavors. After experimenting with a few, I came up with the following method, which works nicely with these flavored tea bags. Cinnamon was a favorite of mine and several friends. It also mixes easily with other teas and is great blended with apple juice. Add some club soda to a glass for a sparkling cooler. For a real treat, make milk shakes using vanilla ice cream. Just use the tea as you would the milk in a regular shake. This tea is great served after dinner.

4 cups water
4 regular-size cinnamon-flavored tea bags
$1/2$ cup granulated sugar

1. Bring 2 cups of the water to a gentle boil in a small saucepan. Add the tea bags, cover, and remove from the heat. Let steep for 12 minutes.

2. Remove the tea bags without squeezing them. Add the sugar and stir until completely dissolved. Add the remaining 2 cups cold water, stir, and pour into a 1-quart container.

3. Let cool, then chill and serve over ice.

➤ MAKES 1 QUART

polly's spiced
iced tea mix

Polly Cooper is thought to be the best architectural firm marketer in North Carolina. But I believe that her true passion is food. Here's her recipe for a quick single glass. Keep a container of this tea mix at your desk.

1 cup orange-flavored powdered breakfast drink mix
1 cup instant iced tea mix with lemon and sugar
$\frac{1}{4}$ teaspoon ground cloves
$\frac{1}{4}$ teaspoon ground cinnamon

1. In a medium-size bowl, stir together the powdered breakfast drink mix, tea mix, cloves, and cinnamon. Transfer to an airtight container.

2. To serve, stir 2 teaspoons of the mix into 8 ounces of cold water until dissolved. Serve over ice.

➤ MAKES ENOUGH MIX FOR ABOUT TWENTY-FOUR 8-OUNCE SERVINGS

chamomile iced tea

Chamomile has long been valued for its soothing, relaxing, and reviving character. A daisylike flower, chamomile is used to make a tisane rather than a true tea. Normally thought of as a warm tea, chamomile is surprisingly delicious when iced. The trick is to make it strong enough, and this recipe does.

8 cups cold water

6 regular-size chamomile tea bags

$1/2$ cup granulated sugar

1. In a small saucepan, bring 2 cups of the water to a slow boil. Add the tea bags, cover, and remove from the heat. Let steep for 15 minutes.

2. Remove the tea bags without squeezing them.

3. Pour the steeped tea into a 2-quart heatproof container. Add the sugar and remaining 6 cups cold water and stir or shake until the sugar is dissolved.

4. Let cool, then chill and serve over ice.

➤ MAKES 2 QUARTS

spearmint iced tea

Spearmint grows like wildfire with little or no attention. If you've never planted spearmint, put a plant or two near your back door, then don't be afraid to use it in all types of recipes. It's unbelievable the zing fresh mint adds to even the simplest of recipes.

8 cups cold water

7 regular-size tea bags

12 sprigs fresh spearmint

Zest of 3 lemons

1 1/2 cups granulated sugar

1 cup freshly squeezed lemon juice (about 6 lemons; don't even think of using bottled)

1. Bring 1 quart of the water to a boil in a medium-size saucepan. Remove from the heat and add the tea bags, spearmint, and zest. Let steep for 15 minutes.

2. Strain through a fine-mesh strainer into a 2-quart heatproof container. Add the sugar, lemon juice, and remaining 1 quart cold water and stir or shake until the sugar is dissolved.

3. Let cool, then chill and serve over ice.

➤ MAKES 2 QUARTS

Use a vegetable peeler to remove the zest of the lemons. Try to avoid the white pith, which can be bitter.

menthe poivrée tea

Oui, peppermint iced tea. This method will work with any fresh mint, but peppermint is a real kicker. This recipe is easily doubled.

4 cups water
5 regular-size tea bags
$^3/_4$ cup granulated sugar
5 sprigs fresh peppermint or any other mint
$^1/_2$ small lemon
Fresh peppermint or other mint leaves for garnish

1. Bring the water to a slow boil in a medium-size saucepan. Add the tea bags, cover, and remove from the heat. Let steep for 10 minutes.

2. Remove the tea bags without squeezing them. Add the sugar and mint. Juice the lemon, adding the juice and the rind to the tea. Cover and let steep for 25 to 30 minutes.

3. Stir to make certain the sugar is dissolved, then strain through a fine-mesh strainer into a 1-quart container.

4. Chill and serve over ice, garnished with a mint leaf.

➤ MAKES 1 QUART

pineapple-lemon-mint iced tea

Pineapple has a natural affinity for tea. Here pineapple juice is combined with the gold standards of lemon and mint, creating a blissful experience.

5 cups cold water

6 regular-size tea bags

3 lemons, seeded and cut into $^1/_2$-inch-thick slices

1 $^1/_2$ cups fresh mint leaves, torn

One 12-ounce can frozen pineapple juice concentrate, thawed

1 cup granulated sugar

2 teaspoons pure vanilla extract

1 teaspoon pure almond extract

1. Bring 2 cups of the water to a gentle boil in a small saucepan. Add the tea bags, lemon slices, and mint. Cover, remove from the heat, and let steep for 20 minutes.

2. Meanwhile, combine the pineapple juice concentrate, remaining 3 cups water, sugar, vanilla, and almond extract in a 2-quart container. Strain the steeped tea through a fine-mesh strainer and add to the pineapple liquid. Stir or shake until the sugar is dissolved.

3. Let cool, then chill and serve over ice.

➤ MAKES ABOUT 2 QUARTS

pineapple tea cooler

Herbal tea infusions are officially known as tisanes. Tisanes are popular hot "teas" touting various tastes and healing effects. Some work well iced, giving you the option to "chill" your way to passion, calmness, or an energy kick. When experimenting with iced tisanes, remember to make the base concentrate strong.

11 cups cold water
6 regular-size hibiscus and rose hips tea bags, such as Celestial
    Seasonings Red Zinger
One 12-ounce can frozen pineapple juice concentrate, thawed

1. In a small saucepan, bring 3 cups of the water to a gentle boil. Add the tea bags, cover, and remove from the heat. Let steep for 15 minutes.

2. Remove the tea bags without squeezing them.

3. Meanwhile, in a 3-quart container, stir the pineapple juice concentrate into the remaining 8 cups water. Add the steeped tea and stir.

4. Let cool, then chill and serve over ice.

➤ MAKES ABOUT 3 QUARTS

lemon-ginger iced tea

Serendipity 3, New York City's most renowned dessert emporium, is famous for its Frozen Hot Chocolate and celebrities' kids' birthday parties. The inspiration for this "tea" came from a visit to this incredible ice cream palace.

8 cups water

2 lemons

1 cup peeled and thinly sliced fresh ginger (about 6 ounces unpeeled ginger)

1/4 cup honey

1/4 cup turbinado or granulated sugar

Cracked ice

Lime wedges for garnish

1. In a medium-size saucepan, bring the water to a boil. Cut the lemons in half and juice them into the boiling water. Add the lemon rinds to the water along with the ginger. Reduce the heat to a simmer, cover, and cook for 10 minutes. Remove from the heat and let steep for an additional 10 minutes, keeping the pan covered.

2. Strain the liquid through a fine-mesh strainer into a 2-quart heatproof container. Add the honey and sugar and stir or shake to combine.

3. Let cool, then chill. Serve over lots of cracked ice, garnished with a lime wedge.

➤ MAKES 2 QUARTS

Use a spoon to easily and safely peel fresh ginger.

lime iced tea

I have no clue where I got this recipe. So thanks to whoever sent it my way. It's cooling and calming on a sweltering summer afternoon.

7 cups cold water
6 regular-size tea bags
1 cup granulated sugar
One 6-ounce can frozen limeade concentrate, thawed
Lime wedges for garnish (optional)

1. Bring 4 cups of the water to a boil in a medium-size saucepan. Add the tea bags, cover, and remove from the heat. Let steep for 5 minutes.

2. Meanwhile, place the sugar and limeade concentrate in a 2-quart heat-proof container.

3. Remove the tea bags without squeezing them.

4. Pour the steeped tea into the container and add the remaining 3 cups cold water. Stir or shake to combine.

5. Let cool, then chill. Serve over ice, garnished with a lime wedge if desired.

➤ MAKES 2 QUARTS

Add a shot of sour mash whiskey and crushed fresh mint leaves to each serving, and you have a perfect cocktail for a Kentucky Derby party.

wild sweet orange iced tea

Another herbal infusion, this tea is a great mixer. Add a shot of an orange-flavored liqueur for a good relaxing moment. There are many brands of orange-flavored tea on the market. I use Tazo.

4 cups cold water
5 regular-size wild sweet orange herbal infusion tea bags
$1/2$ cup granulated sugar

1. Bring 2 cups of the water to a slow boil in a small saucepan. Add the tea bags, cover, and remove from the heat. Let steep for 12 minutes.

2. Remove the tea bags without squeezing them. Add the sugar, stirring until dissolved.

3. Pour into a 1-quart container and add the remaining 2 cups cold water.

4. Let cool, then chill and serve over ice.

➤ MAKES 1 QUART

bimini island
iced tea

This tea is an absolute taste of the tropics. Throw in some coconut rum, and Hemingway might show up for a drink.

> 1 quart Wild Sweet Orange Iced Tea (page 43), made without the sugar, chilled
>
> One 32-ounce bottle pineapple-coconut juice
>
> Pineapple sticks and star fruit slices for garnish

1. Combine the brewed tea and pineapple-coconut juice in a 2-quart pitcher.

2. Chill and serve over ice, garnished with the exotic fruit.

➤ MAKES 2 QUARTS

citrus iced tea

Lemon wedges and juice are commonplace with iced tea, but a little orange juice and a few cloves will delight you on an early fall day. This recipe needs an extra hour to infuse the cloves in water, so allow for that in your preparation. And, please, don't try this with ground cloves.

6 cloves

8 cups cold water

9 regular-size tea bags

1/2 cup freshly squeezed orange juice

1/2 cup freshly squeezed lemon juice (about 3 lemons; don't even think of using bottled)

1 1/2 cups granulated sugar

1. To infuse the cloves, combine them with 2 cups of the water in a small saucepan. Bring the mixture to a boil, remove from the heat, and let steep for at least 45 minutes, preferably 1 hour.

2. Bring 2 cups of the remaining water to a gentle boil in a small saucepan. Add the tea bags, cover, and remove from the heat. Let steep for 5 to 10 minutes.

3. Remove the tea bags without squeezing them.

4. Strain the clove water through a fine-mesh strainer into a 2-quart container. Add the steeped tea, orange juice, lemon juice, and sugar. Stir or shake until the sugar is dissolved. Add the remaining 4 cups cold water and shake or stir to combine.

5. Let cool, then chill and serve over ice.

➤ MAKES ABOUT 2 QUARTS

iced mango tea with lemon syrup

This interesting tea combination is wonderful for picnics. The lemon syrup gives everybody a choice about the final flavor of his or her tea.

7 $1/3$ cups cold water

6 regular-size mango-flavored tea bags

$1/3$ cup freshly squeezed lemon juice (about 2 lemons; don't use bottled)

$1/2$ cup granulated sugar

Cracked ice

Fresh mint sprigs for garnish (optional)

1. Bring 7 cups of the water to a gentle boil in a medium-size saucepan. Add the tea bags, cover, and remove from the heat. Let steep for 10 minutes.

2. Remove the tea bags without squeezing them. Let cool completely at room temperature, then refrigerate.

3. While the tea is steeping, combine the lemon juice, sugar, and remaining $1/3$ cup water in a small nonreactive saucepan. Cover and cook over low heat until the sugar is completely dissolved. Uncover and bring to a boil over medium-high heat. Remove from the heat and let cool completely.

4. To serve, pour the steeped tea into tall glasses and stir 1 tablespoon of the lemon syrup (or to taste) into each glass. Fill the glasses with cracked ice. Garnish with a mint sprig, if desired.

➤ MAKES ABOUT 2 QUARTS

fred's apple cider iced tea

Some things are best left simple. This tea, fried chicken, and a slice of sweet potato pie are perfect partners for a tailgate party. A shot of rum in your glass will take the chill off the fall air.

2 cups apple cider
1 quart Sweet Tea (page 21)

1. Combine the cider and tea.
2. Chill and serve over ice.

➤ MAKES 1½ QUARTS

berry-spice
iced tea

I am enamored of black currant tea. It has a unique sweetness that mellows the tannins of the tea. Black currant tea mixes with a host of flavors, but cranberries and black currants have a regal quality when paired together.

3 cups water

3 regular-size black currant-flavored tea bags or 3 teaspoons
   black currant-flavored tea leaves

3 cinnamon sticks, each about 3 inches long

10 cloves

$\frac{1}{3}$ cup granulated sugar

$1\frac{1}{2}$ cups cranberry juice cocktail

1 tablespoon freshly squeezed lemon juice (don't use bottled)

Thinly sliced lemon for garnish

1. In a small saucepan, bring the water to a gentle boil. Add the tea bags or loose tea, cover, and remove from the heat. Let steep for 10 minutes.

2. Remove the tea bags without squeezing or strain out the leaves using a fine-mesh strainer. Add the cinnamon sticks, cloves, and sugar, cover, and let cool to room temperature.

3. Strain the liquid through a fine-mesh strainer into a pitcher. Add the cranberry juice and lemon juice and stir to combine.

4. Chill, then serve over ice, garnished with a lemon slice.

➤ MAKES A LITTLE MORE THAN 1 QUART

iced tea
spritzers

Make a soda out of tea? Why not? Here are a few playful spritzers for you to enjoy. Do not feel confined by the carbonated beverages suggested. They truly are just a starting point. Experiment with your favorite soft drinks and sparkling waters.

carbonated classic iced tea

Americans love carbonated soda. I think you'll find this combination of iced tea and soda tangy and refreshing. This recipe is easily doubled.

> 3 cups water
> 6 regular-size tea bags
> $^1/_2$ cup granulated sugar
> Chilled lemon-lime soda, as needed
> Thinly sliced lemon, lime, or orange for garnish

1. Bring the water to a gentle boil in a small saucepan. Add the tea bags, cover, and remove from the heat. Let steep for 10 minutes.

2. Remove the tea bags without squeezing them.

3. Pour the tea concentrate into a 2½-quart heatproof pitcher. Add the sugar, stirring to dissolve. Let cool, then chill.

4. When ready to serve, divide the tea among 6 tall tea glasses filled with ice. Top with soda and garnish with a fruit slice.

➤ MAKES 6 SERVINGS

simple ginger tea

Okay, so you love that ginger flavor but don't want to work hard to get it? Here's your quick and simple answer. If your part of the country has an artisan soda bottler, give its ginger ale a try. I'm lucky in having access to Blenheim Ginger Ale. This South Carolina company produces old-fashioned ginger ale that makes this tea sing. Seek out a similar bottler in your neck of the woods, or give Blenheim a call at 800-270-9344.

2 cups unsweetened brewed black tea. chilled

1 cup freshly squeezed orange juice

3 tablespoons freshly squeezed lemon juice (don't use bottled)

$^1/_4$ cup superfine sugar

2 cups ginger ale. chilled

Orange slices for garnish (optional)

Lemon slices for garnish (optional)

1. Blend the tea, orange juice, lemon juice, and sugar together in a 2-quart pitcher. Mix well, stirring until the sugar is dissolved. Slowly pour in the ginger ale and stir to combine.

2. Serve immediately over ice, garnished with an orange and lemon slice if desired.

➤ MAKES 4 SERVINGS

cheerwine spritzer

Cheerwine is an original. First bottled by the Carolina Beverage Corporation of Salisbury, North Carolina, this burgundy-colored, cherry-based cola has devotees from Virginia to Florida. Don't worry if it is not in your store. It is easily ordered online, or you can substitute Dr. Brown's Black Cherry Soda. It won't be the same, but it will be close.

4 cups unsweetened brewed black tea, chilled

Two 6-ounce cans pineapple juice

4 cups Cheerwine, chilled

One 10-ounce jar maraschino cherries with stems for garnish

1. In a $2\frac{1}{2}$-quart container, combine the brewed tea and pineapple juice. Keep cold until ready to serve.

2. Add the Cheerwine to the tea mixture and serve immediately over ice, garnished with a cherry.

➤ MAKES 8 TO 10 SERVINGS

Cheerwine can be ordered on the Internet at www.cheerwine.com.

Dr. Brown's can be ordered at www.popsoda.com.

green tea–passion fruit spritzer

Green tea pairs well with a multitude of flavors, and passion fruit is one of the best. An ounce of amaretto, the liqueur of love, won't hurt either. This recipe can be easily doubled.

4 cups cold water
3 regular-size green tea bags
$^1/_3$ cup honey
2 cups passion fruit nectar (available in health food stores and larger supermarkets)
Chilled sparkling water, as needed
Fresh mint sprigs for garnish (optional)

1. Bring 2 cups of the water to a gentle boil in a small saucepan. Add the tea bags, cover, and remove from the heat. Let steep for 15 minutes.

2. Remove the tea bags without squeezing them. Stir in the honey until dissolved.

3. Pour the sweetened tea into a 2-quart heatproof container. Add the remaining 2 cups cold water and the passion fruit nectar. Let cool, then chill.

4. When ready to serve, fill 6 tall glasses with ice. Fill each glass three-quarters full with tea and top off with sparkling water. Garnish with a mint sprig, if desired.

➤ MAKES 8 SERVINGS

tea for
company

There is nothing more hospitable than offering company a glass of iced tea. The iced teas included in this chapter are extraordinary and best reserved for special occasions with friends and family. A mixture of punches and teas, all of these can be easily doubled or even tripled to satisfy a crowd, from a wedding reception to a "pig-picking." If a stronger libation is warranted, check out "For Adults Only" for punches that might also be appropriate for your occasion.

sparkling
strawberry tea

A Mother's Day luncheon, bridal shower, or graduation party blessed with this tea will require the host to be ready to hand out the recipe—or maybe it's best to hold the secret close. "Spring in a glass" describes this libation. Lemonade can be substituted for the limeade, and the mint is up to you. If you need a sweeter tea for the children, top it off with lemon-lime soda instead of sparkling water.

One 10-ounce package frozen strawberries in syrup, thawed
6 cups water
3 family-size tea bags
$1/2$ cup granulated sugar
One 6-ounce can frozen limeade concentrate, thawed
Fresh mint sprigs (optional)
Two 1-liter bottles sparkling water, chilled
Sliced fresh strawberries for garnish

1. In a blender or food processor, process the thawed strawberries until smooth. Set aside.

2. Bring the water to a gentle boil in a medium-size saucepan. Add the tea bags, cover, and remove from the heat. Let steep for 10 minutes.

3. Remove the tea bags without squeezing them. Stir in the sugar until dissolved. Stir in the limeade and strawberry puree.

4. Pour the tea into a 2-quart container and add mint sprigs if desired. Let cool. Remove the mint, then chill.

5. When ready to serve, pour the tea mixture into a punch bowl large enough to handle the tea plus the sparkling water. Slowly add the sparkling water. Serve over ice. If desired, add sliced strawberries to the punch bowl or each glass for garnish.

➤ MAKES ABOUT 1 GALLON; 12 REGULAR SERVINGS OR 24 PUNCH-CUP SERVINGS

charleston tea plantation wedding punch

Charleston, South Carolina, was once a hub of tea plantations. Most fell victim to the War for Southern Independence and bad economies. Thanks to Mack Fleming and William B. Hall, growing tea in this country is once again a reality. The Charleston Tea Plantation on Wadmalaw Island produces the only tea grown in the United States. This tea is sold under the American Classic Tea label. Look in specialty stores for this brand. The tea is deep in flavor and quality, equal to any tea grown in the world. This punch is from the company's recipe files.

4 cups unsweetened brewed American Classic Tea or any other
   black tea, chilled
4 cups apple juice, chilled
2 cups pineapple juice, chilled
Two 1-liter bottles club soda, chilled
2 oranges, sliced and seeded
2 lemons, sliced and seeded
10 sprigs fresh mint for garnish

1. Combine the brewed tea, apple juice, and pineapple juice in a 1-gallon container and refrigerate until ready to serve.

2. Immediately before serving, combine the tea mixture with the club soda and fruit slices in a large punch bowl. Add the mint sprigs and serve over ice.

➤ MAKES 3½ QUARTS; 25 TO 30 PUNCH-CUP SERVINGS

thoroughbred iced tea

On a sales trip to western Kentucky twenty-some-odd years ago, I ate in a wonderful roadside diner whose name totally escapes me. The iced tea there was unique, but the recipe was a secret. All I got out of the waitress was that the two "secret" ingredients were white grape juice and lemonade mix. After a few failed efforts, this recipe comes pretty close. It's great for a cookout.

8 cups water

3 family-size tea bags

2 cups granulated sugar

One 23-ounce envelope unsweetened lemonade-flavored
   drink mix

2 1/2 cups white grape juice. chilled

1. In a medium-size saucepan, bring the water to a gentle boil. Add the tea bags, cover, and remove from the heat. Let steep for 10 minutes.

2. Meanwhile, in a 2½-quart container, combine the sugar, lemonade drink mix, and grape juice.

3. Remove the tea bags without squeezing them and pour the tea into the sugar mixture. Stir or shake to dissolve the sugar.

4. Let cool, then chill and serve over ice.

➤ MAKES 2½ QUARTS

"teatotaler's" sangria

Those who totally abstain from alcohol are known as teetotalers. This festive sangria, its name a play on words, is a remarkable foil for a hot afternoon cookout or when entertaining Southern Baptists (I can say that because I am one). Teetotaler or not, you'll enjoy this one.

3 oranges, sliced and seeded

3 lemons, sliced and seeded

3 limes, cut into wedges

$^1/_2$ cup seasonal fruit such as cherries, blackberries, or strawberries, sliced or left whole

3 cups unsweetened brewed green tea, chilled

4 cups all-natural cranberry-peach juice, chilled

One 6-ounce can pineapple juice

1 cup sparkling white grape juice, chilled

One 16-ounce package frozen peach slices, not thawed

1. In a 2½-quart glass container, combine the orange and lemon slices, lime wedges, and seasonal fruit. Pour the brewed green tea, cranberry-peach juice, and pineapple juice into the container.

2. Just before serving, stir in the grape juice and float the frozen peach slices on top. Try to get some fruit with each serving.

➤ MAKES SLIGHTLY MORE THAN 2 QUARTS; 8 TO 10 SERVINGS

grenadine tea

This combination is grand for family reunions that have a large number of kids and wish-they-were-kids. Adding the grenadine at the last minute before serving creates a cool effect.

---

8 cups water

6 regular-size tea bags

1 1/2 cups freshly squeezed lemon juice (about 9 lemons; don't even think of using bottled)

2 1/2 cups pineapple juice

1 cup grenadine

One 10-ounce jar maraschino cherries without stems, drained

Lemon slices for garnish (optional)

Fresh mint sprigs for garnish (optional)

---

1. Bring the water to a gentle boil in a medium-size saucepan. Add the tea bags, cover, and remove from the heat. Let steep for 5 to 10 minutes.

2. Remove the tea bags without squeezing them. Let the steeped tea cool.

3. In a 4-quart container, combine the lemon juice and pineapple juice. Add the steeped tea, grenadine, and cherries. Don't stir until ready to serve.

4. Serve over ice, garnished with a lemon slice and mint sprig if desired.

➤ MAKES ABOUT 3½ QUARTS; 14 TO 16 SERVINGS

no-alcohol tea and fruit punch

Not all Southern tea-based punches really need a "punch." This one is as appropriate for a child's party as it is for a wedding reception. If you want to adjust the ingredients to your own taste, go right ahead.

One 12-ounce can frozen orange juice concentrate, thawed
One 6-ounce can frozen lemonade concentrate, thawed
12 cups water
8 cups unsweetened strong brewed black tea, chilled
3 cups granulated sugar
1 cup grenadine (optional)
$1/2$ gallon lemon or lime sherbet or sorbet, slightly softened
Five 1-liter bottles ginger ale, chilled
Fresh strawberries, hulled, for garnish (optional)

1. In a 2-gallon container, combine the orange juice and lemonade concentrates. Add the water, brewed tea, sugar, and grenadine, if using. Stir to blend. Cover and chill for 12 hours.

2. Just before serving, spoon your choice of sherbet or sorbet into a chilled punch bowl. Add the tea mixture. Slowly pour in the ginger ale, carefully stirring to mix. Garnish with the whole strawberries, if desired. Serve over ice.

➤ MAKES ABOUT 3 GALLONS; 50 PUNCH-CUP SERVINGS

salem college
iced tea

Every small college in the South has a special "reception tea" served at reunions and commencements. Salem College is in Winston-Salem, North Carolina, next to my hometown of Greensboro. I pulled this recipe from my mother's files. How authentic it is could be debated, as most of these recipes are closely guarded secrets. But it is a damn good tea.

8 cups water
4 sprigs fresh mint
10 cloves
2 family-size tea bags
Juice of 8 lemons
Juice of 6 oranges
One 46-ounce can pineapple juice
2 cups granulated sugar
Fresh fruit slices for garnish (optional)

1. In a medium-size saucepan, combine the water, mint, and cloves. Bring to a gentle boil, reduce the heat to medium-low, and simmer for 10 to 15 minutes.

2. Remove from the heat and add the tea bags. Cover and let steep for 10 to 15 minutes.

3. Strain the tea mixture through a fine-mesh strainer into a 1-gallon container. Add the fruit juices and sugar. Stir or shake until the sugar is dissolved. Let cool, then chill.

4. Serve over ice, garnished with fruit slices if desired.

➤ MAKES SLIGHTLY LESS THAN 1 GALLON; 20 PUNCH-CUP SERVINGS

outer banks fall tea

Late September and early October have the most agreeable weather for sitting on the almost deserted beaches on the Outer Banks of North Carolina, doing absolutely nothing. Fresh apple cider is available and, when mixed with tea and ginger ale, offers an exquisite drink to enjoy the calm. Remember, the holidays are looming, so take some time and "chill."

2 cups unsweetened brewed black tea, chilled

1 quart fresh apple cider

$^1/_4$ cup freshly squeezed lemon juice (about 1 $^1/_2$ lemons; don't use bottled)

One 1-liter bottle ginger ale, chilled

1. Mix the brewed tea, apple cider, and lemon juice together in a 1$^1/_2$-quart container. Keep chilled until ready to serve.

2. Pour the tea mixture into a 2$^1/_2$-quart pitcher and, just before serving, slowly pour in the ginger ale, then gently stir. Serve over ice.

➤ MAKES ABOUT 2$^1/_2$ QUARTS; 10 SERVINGS

For a single serving, fill a tall glass two-thirds full with the tea mixture, then top with ginger ale and add ice.

strange
ways
with tea

These iced teas cross some cultural boundaries. Of course, there are some as retro as an old-fashioned ice cream soda. A smoothie with tea adds an extra kick of healthy ingredients. This is the chapter to read when you are really ready for an adventure.

cha yen
(thai iced tea)

If the sometimes blistering heat of Thai food has you eating cautiously, you are missing a wonderful cuisine. The Thais drink this supersweet, lightly spiced beverage to calm their foods. *Cha yen,* or "cold tea," as it translates, is from a blend of black tea, vanilla, cinnamon, and star anise. This special tea was once found only in Asian markets, but now it is available in the Asian or Thai section of larger supermarkets.

There is a debate about which milk product to use in *cha yen.* In all the Thai restaurants in Manhattan's Chinatown where I've tasted this cool treat, sweetened condensed milk is mixed with the tea, then a tablespoon of evaporated milk or half-and-half is floated on top. Some authorities on Thai cooking use sugar and half-and-half to make *cha yen.* One Thai cook suggested half condensed milk and half evaporated milk. No matter which combination you choose, there's no other beverage that works as well with the foods of Thailand.

4 cups water

$1/2$ cup Thai tea leaves

One 10-ounce can sweetened condensed milk

Cracked or crushed ice

$1/4$ cup milk, half-and-half, or evaporated milk

1. Bring the water to a boil in a medium-size saucepan. Add the tea leaves and remove from the heat. This tea floats to the top, and you will need to stir the tea. Do this quickly. When all of the tea leaves are wet, cover and let steep for 5 minutes.

2. Strain the tea through a fine-mesh strainer into a heatproof container. Stir in the condensed milk until blended. Chill thoroughly.

3. When time to serve, fill 4 glasses with cracked or crushed ice. Pour the tea into the glasses and top with 1 tablespoon of milk, half-and-half, or evaporated milk.

➤ MAKES 4 SERVINGS

tea smoothie

Just when you think smoothies have lost their moment, along comes a heat wave, and we rejuvenate the beverage. This simple recipe is open to your interpretation. The tea can be flavored to accommodate any kind of yogurt. An orange-flavored tea and French vanilla yogurt returns me to the days of Creamsicles. Regular tea with lemon yogurt makes a creamy concoction for the pool or beach.

2 cups unsweetened brewed tea. chilled

1 cup lemon yogurt

Lemon slices for garnish (optional)

1. In a blender, process the tea and yogurt for 20 seconds.
2. Chill for 20 to 30 minutes.
3. Serve in well-chilled glasses, garnished with a lemon slice if desired.

➤ MAKES 4 SERVINGS

Here are some interesting variations:
- Cinnamon tea and apple-cinnamon yogurt
- Mixed-berry green tea with raspberry yogurt
- Any flavored tea with the same flavor yogurt for a bold taste

iced *chai*

Chai is the Hindu word for tea. The recipe was a royal secret in the ancient courts of India and Siam, and legend says that *chai* was invented by a king. The offering of a beverage to guests in one's home is mandatory etiquette in the region. *Chai*, with its creamy texture and flavor, is the number one choice in India.

Chai hit the United States a few years ago, and although it has not generated the same craze as coffee, it has a loyal following and is served in coffee bars and upscale specialty houses. This recipe is a simple version, but tasteful and true in spirit to a spiced *chai* you might find in Southwest Asia. And it's a lot cheaper than that found in most coffee bars.

2 cups water
1/4 cup Darjeeling or Ceylon tea leaves or 5 regular-size tea bags
1 cup milk
1 cup half-and-half (lowfat is okay)
1/4 teaspoon ground cardamom
3 cloves, crushed
2 black peppercorns, crushed
1/8 teaspoon ground cinnamon
1/8 teaspoon ground ginger
1/4 cup sweetened condensed milk

1. In a medium-size saucepan, bring the water to a gentle boil. Stir the tea leaves into the water. Reduce the heat to medium-low and simmer for 5 minutes. Add the milk, half-and-half, cardamom, cloves, peppercorns, cinnamon, and ginger. Increase the heat and bring to a full boil, being careful not to let the milk boil over.

2. Remove from the heat and strain through a fine-mesh strainer into a heatproof container. Stir in the condensed milk.

3. Let cool, then chill and serve over ice.

➤ MAKES 4 SERVINGS

To crush the peppercorns and cloves, use the edge of a sauté pan. For even fresher, bolder flavors, use whole cardamom seeds ground in a spice grinder or mortar and pestle. For a variation, try adding 1/4 teaspoon pure vanilla extract with the condensed milk.

tea and
ice cream soda

Maybe this sounds nuts to you, but give it a try before judging this cooling concoction. Although regular tea will work, the strong brew below gives this soda more presence. Also try this recipe with a flavored tea. Raspberry, peach, blackberry, and mixed-berry green tea all work nicely.

1 cup boiling water

2 regular-size tea bags

Vanilla, mint chocolate chip, or strawberry ice cream

Chilled ginger ale, as needed

4 maraschino cherries with stems for garnish (optional)

Whipped cream (optional)

1. Pour the boiling water over the tea bags in a heatproof container and let steep for 10 minutes.

2. Remove the tea bags without squeezing them. Let the tea cool to room temperature.

3. When ready to serve, place scoops (at least 2 big scoops) of ice cream in the bottom of 4 soda glasses. Divide the tea equally among the 4 glasses. Top off with ginger ale. Serve with straws and long-handled spoons. Garnish with a cherry and whipped cream, if desired.

➤ MAKES 4 SERVINGS

i didn't want a V-8 iced tea

A chef from Australia inspired this seemingly strange tea. Tomato and tea may sound bizarre, but it is quite cooling on a hot day. The sun-dried tomatoes add a hint of smokiness.

One 14 1/2-ounce can diced tomatoes
6 to 8 sun-dried tomatoes (not oil-packed), to your taste
6 cups cold water
1 tablespoon Ceylon tea leaves

1. In a medium-size saucepan, bring the canned tomatoes, sun-dried tomatoes, 2 cups of the water, and tea leaves to a boil. Cover, remove from the heat, and let steep for 10 minutes.

2. Strain through a fine-mesh strainer into a 1 1/2-quart container, pressing firmly on the solids to release all their juices. Add the remaining 4 cups water and stir.

3. Chill thoroughly, then serve over plenty of ice.

➤ MAKES ABOUT 1 QUART; 4 TO 6 SERVINGS

Be sure not to use oil-packed sun-dried tomatoes. The oil will destroy the delicacy of this tea. It is great for brunch and takes well to vodka and gin.

bay leaf—lemon balm iced tea

Craig Claiborne changed many thoughts on food during his reign at the *New York Times.* Claiborne was born in the South and stayed true to his Southern roots in many respects. A bay leaf tea that he used for a variety of purposes inspired this recipe. Be sure to add the soda when instructed, so the carbonation will be gone by the time you serve it.

2 cups water

8 large bay leaves

6 fresh lemon balm leaves

1 family-size tea bag

One 12-ounce can Dr. Brown's Cel-Ray Soda, chilled

1. Combine the water, bay leaves, and lemon balm in a medium-size saucepan and bring to a boil. Add the tea bag, cover, and remove from the heat. Let steep for 15 minutes.

2. Strain through a fine-mesh strainer into a 1-quart container and add the soda.

3. Let cool, then chill and serve over ice.

➤ MAKES 3 OR 4 SERVINGS

Dr. Brown's Cel-Ray
Soda can be ordered at
www.popsoda.com.

for
adults
only

As the name implies, these are not iced teas that can be shared with the kids. All contain alcohol. Some of my personal favorites are in this chapter, mainly because of the memories they evoke for me.

beach bourbon slush

Bunko is a game that men probably don't want to know anything about. Taken more seriously by the womenfolk in my neighborhood than any Thursday night poker game, I have always suspected that it is the gossip and husband bashing that really makes Bunko night special. This recipe, served by Edna Ruth Hadley one Bunko night, deserves widespread attention. It is an icy refresher that has become *de rigueur* during my family's annual trek to the South Carolina coast. I can't imagine a day at the beach without this silky syrup. It goes down pretty well on the back porch at home, too. Make sure you serve it in chilled glasses.

2 cups unsweetened brewed black tea
5 cups water
1 pint Jack Daniel's Old No. 7
$^1/_4$ cup granulated sugar
One 12-ounce can frozen lemonade concentrate, thawed
One 6-ounce can frozen orange juice concentrate, thawed
Chilled ginger ale, as needed

1. Combine the brewed tea, water, Jack Daniel's, sugar, and lemonade and orange juice concentrates in a 9 x 13-inch baking pan or any container large enough to hold the mixture that is only a few inches deep. Place in the freezer. About once every 45 minutes, stir the blend with a fork. Continue this for a couple of hours, until the mixture has the consistency of a granita: icy, slushy, and granular.

2. To serve, use an ice cream scoop or large, heavy spoon to fill a glass two-thirds full with the frozen tea. Top with some ginger ale. Don't stir. Let the ginger ale coagulate with the frozen tea, then drink up.

➤ NUMBER OF SERVINGS DEPENDS ON WHO'S DRINKING

bourbon-tea punch

My father's best business associate friend retired to Panama City, Florida. This was his house special summer sipper. Since he spent most of his career in Louisville, Kentucky, well, bourbon just has a major role in this tea.

2 cups water

3 regular-size tea bags

3 cups bourbon

2 cups freshly squeezed orange juice

1 cup freshly squeezed lemon juice (about 6 lemons; don't use bottled)

1 cup Grand Marnier or other orange-flavored liqueur

1 cup granulated sugar

Two 1-liter bottles club soda, chilled

1. Bring the water to a gentle boil in a small saucepan. Add the tea bags, cover, and remove from the heat. Let steep for 15 minutes.

2. Remove the tea bags without squeezing them.

3. Pour the steeped tea into a 2½-quart heatproof container. Add the bourbon, orange juice, lemon juice, liqueur, and sugar. Stir or shake until the sugar is dissolved.

4. Chill thoroughly.

5. To serve as a punch, pour into a punch bowl and add the club soda. For individual drinks, use 1 part tea-bourbon mixture to 2 parts club soda per glass.

➤ MAKES ABOUT 12 REGULAR OR 24 TO 30 PUNCH-CUP SERVINGS

moo u. tea

North Carolina State University (NCSU), my alma mater, was referred to as Moo U. by the rival colleges because of our world-famous agricultural school. As guys, we really didn't care. Raleigh, the city where NCSU is located, is blessed with three all-girl colleges, which more than made up for the jabs. The problem was, most of the girls from these colleges drank beer or daiquiris. One night, for an impromptu party before exams, all that was to be had was gin and no limes. Iced tea was always in somebody's refrigerator, and if you had gin, you had tonic. Being the ever-imaginative bartender, I gave birth to Moo U. Tea. I've refined this tea over the years and probably should rename it, but the memories are just too good.

3 cups Sweet Tea (page 21), chilled
$^1/_2$ cup freshly squeezed lemon juice (about 3 lemons; don't use bottled)
$^1/_2$ cup orange juice (freshly squeezed is best)
1 pint gin
Maraschino cherries with stems for garnish

1. Combine the Sweet Tea, lemon juice, orange juice, and gin in a 1½-quart container. Chill for at least 30 minutes, longer if possible. (This can even be put together the day before.)

2. Serve over ice in old-fashioned glasses, garnished with a cherry.

➤ MAKES ABOUT 6 SERVINGS

For a less potent drink, fill tall glasses with ice. Fill the glass one third full with the gin mixture and top with tonic water. Garnish with a cherry.

To serve as a punch, place the gin mixture in a large punch bowl and add two 1-liter bottles of tonic water. Garnish with cherries. A gallon-size wide-mouth jar works if the occasion doesn't warrant a punch bowl or you just don't want to play bartender.

chatham
artillery punch

Thanks to John Berendt's book *Midnight in the Garden of Good and Evil,* millions of us "outsiders" have become acquainted with the social habits of the city of Savannah, Georgia. "What are you drinking?" comes quickly after any introduction or arrival to a party there. In my humble opinion, the folks of Savannah may just have figured out this existence on earth. Life is truly to be lived, not watched.

The city's most famous drink is Chatham Artillery Punch, named after Savannah's elite Civil War militia. Several glasses of this unholy libation will certainly get you involved in living in the here and now. Plan ahead, though. The base for this punch needs to cure for at least two weeks; six is better, and longer is better still. You might want your guests to sign a release before consuming this potent punch.

8 cups cold water
One 4-ounce can gunpowder green tea
Juice of 9 oranges
Juice of 9 lemons
One 1-pound box plus $^1/_2$ cup firmly packed light brown sugar
Two 10-ounce jars maraschino cherries without stems. drained
One 1.5-liter bottle jug-style sweet white wine (Catawba is the
    best)
1 quart light rum
1 quart rye whiskey
1 quart gin
One 25.4-ounce bottle brandy
$^1/_2$ cup Benedictine
Chilled champagne or club soda. as needed

1. Combine the water and tea in a large container; let stand overnight.

2. The next day, stir in the orange and lemon juices and strain through a fine-mesh strainer into a 3-gallon glass container. Add the brown sugar, cherries, jug wine, rum, whiskey, gin, brandy, and Benedictine and mix well.

Cover tightly and set aside in a cool, dark place. Now be patient for at least 2 weeks.

3. Strain the base through a fine-mesh strainer, discarding the solids. Pour the liquid into three 1-gallon containers. Chill.

4. When it is time to serve, pour 1 to 3 gallons of the base into a punch bowl and add 1 bottle of champagne or club soda for each gallon of base used. Add ice and hold on.

➤ MAKES 2½ TO 3 GALLONS OF THE BASE; 100 TO 125 PUNCH-CUP SERVINGS

summertime tea sangria

Sangria is so easy to make, and few beverages refresh like sangria in the summer. This is perfect for a cookout, a neighborhood potluck, or tapas on the porch. Cram as much fruit as you want into the pitcher. Keep the tea and wine amounts in proportion, and you can serve as many folks as need be.

Zest of 1 lemon, taken off in strips (see the sidebar on page 36)

2 lemons, sliced and seeded

2 oranges, sliced and seeded

2 cups grapes

1 cup cherries, or more to taste

1 cup unsweetened brewed black tea

One 750-milliliter bottle fruity red wine

Chilled club soda, as needed

1. In a 2½- to 3-quart container, combine the zest, lemon slices, orange slices, grapes, and cherries. Pour the brewed tea over the fruit, then the wine. Refrigerate.

2. When time to serve, transfer to a punch bowl. Add lots of ice and just enough club soda to give the wine a little effervescence.

➤ MAKES AT LEAST 6 SERVINGS

goombay iced tea

At Potter's Cay, a sliver of land between Nassau and Paradise Island in the Bahamas, you'll find the freshest conch and fish anywhere in the New Providence Island area. This cay is a favorite of the locals, with several shacks "scorching" (cooking the conch with lots of chiles) and "cracking" (batter-frying) conch straight from the boats. Both of these native dishes are super-hot, demanding a cool liquid to wash them down. Along with Kalik, the local beer, this "tea" is a favorite.

Cracked ice
4 cups orange juice (freshly squeezed is best)
4 cups unsweetened brewed tea, chilled
3 tablespoons honey, or more, depending on the sweetness of the orange juice
1 cup golden coconut rum
Orange slices for garnish (optional)

1. Fill a 2½-quart or larger container with cracked ice. Pour in half the orange juice, then half the tea. Add the honey and all the rum. Finish with the remaining orange juice and tea, adding one, then the other. Stir to blend.

2. Pour into chilled glasses filled with ice. Garnish with an orange slice, if desired.

➤ MAKES 8 TO 10 SERVINGS

This tea can also be made into a frozen drink in your blender. Add ice to fill, 1 cup brewed tea, 1 cup orange juice, 1 tablespoon honey, and ¼ cup (or more) coconut rum. Blend, pulsing if needed, to a slushy state, a couple of minutes depending on the power of your blender. Makes 3 or 4 servings.

long island iced tea

Yep, that's right: there's no tea in Long Island iced tea. But as a serious refresher, I couldn't leave it out of my compilation. My Long Island Iced Tea has quite a reputation, so drink one at your own peril.

Cracked ice

$^1/_2$ ounce vodka

$^1/_2$ ounce gin

$^1/_2$ ounce light rum

$^1/_2$ ounce triple sec

$^1/_4$ ounce tequila

1 tablespoon freshly squeezed lemon juice (don't use bottled)

$^3/_4$ cup cola. or more if needed to fill the glass

Ice cubes

Lemon slice for garnish

Fresh mint sprig for garnish

1. Fill a mixing glass or shaker with cracked ice. Add the vodka, gin, rum, triple sec, tequila, and lemon juice. Shake until very cold, then strain into a collins glass filled with ice cubes.

2. Top off with cola, then garnish with a lemon slice and mint sprig. Serve with a straw and an iced-tea spoon.

➤ MAKES 1 DRINK

green tea martini

Cocktails have returned, and none more decisively than the martini. Nor has any cocktail spawned so many variations. The cosmopolitan cocktail got it started, and now we have sextinis, green apple martinis, and French martinis, to name only a few. I sampled a green tea martini in a hot nightspot in lower Manhattan, and although the bartender kept mum on the ingredients, after several attempts, I think I've come pretty close. The research one has to do! Of course, you need chilled martini glasses for this one.

$^3/_4$ cup brewed green tea, sweetened to your taste and chilled
$^3/_4$ cup orange-flavored vodka
Cracked ice
4 small lime wedges

1. Place the green tea and vodka in a cocktail shaker or any jar with a lid. Fill with cracked ice. Shake until very cold, at least 30 seconds.

2. Strain into chilled martini glasses and squeeze a lime wedge into each glass.

➤ MAKES 4 SERVINGS

about the author

Photograph by KAT

Fred Thompson is a food stylist, writer, and recipe developer who trained at the Culinary Institute of America. He lives in New York City and Raleigh, North Carolina, where he writes "The Weekend Gourmet" column for the *News & Observer*. He is also the author of *Lemonade*.

acknowledgments

To Pam Hoenig, an editor who changed my life's direction on January 21. To Susan Byrnes for great photographs, when her life was changed on September 11, and Justin Schwartz. To Toni Allegro, who helps me look good on the page. To Marty Umans. To Elizabeth Van Itallie for the kicking design of both my books. To all the *great* folks at the Harvard Common Press. To my English professor aunt, Dr. Janice Thompson: see, some things did stick! To Linda Johnson, who always thought I had a book in me. And finally, to my computer expert and proofreader, Kat, who let me go insane when necessary.